If It Was a Snake, It Would Have Bit You

Recognizing and Seizing Opportunities

Bonnie Fallin

Copyright © 2020

All rights reserved.

No part of this book may be copied or reproduced, in whole or in part, without the express written permission of the copyright holder and/or publisher.

No liability is assumed for losses or damages, personal, psychological, financial or otherwise, due to the information provided. You are responsible for your own choices, actions, and results.

ISBN-13: 978-1-949003-45-1 print edition
ISBN-13: 978-1-949003-46-8 ebook edition

Waterside Productions
2055 Oxford Ave
Cardiff, CA 92007
www.waterside.com

Printed in the United States of America

Sometimes, opportunities can be all around you- but you can only see obstacles. Bonnie shows you common sense approach that can be used at any age and any stage. The things I could have done if I had this sooner!

Maresa Friedman, Fortune 500 Strategist & Speaker

'Love this book! My copy is highlighted, earmarked and already a permanent member in my library"

Greg S. Reid, Author: Think and Grow Rich series
"How may I be of contribution?"
Greg Reid, Forbes and Inc top rated Keynote Speaker

The Beauty of a Woman

For attractive lips ... Speak with words of kindness.

For lovely eyes ... Seek out the good in people.

For a slimmer figure ... Share your food with the hungry.

For beautiful hair ... Let a child run his or her fingers through it once a day.

For poise ... Walk with the knowledge you'll never walk alone.

People, even more than things, have to be restored, renewed, revived, reclaimed and redeemed ... Never throw out anybody.

Audrey Hepburn

IF IT WAS A SNAKE, IT WOULD HAVE BIT YOU!

Recognizing and Seizing Opportunities

BONNIE FALLIN

TABLE OF CONTENTS

1	The Importance of Deciding What You Want	7
2	What Keeps Us From Getting What We Want	33
3	What Can We Do to Move Toward Success?	51
4	Get Your Life Healthy, So You Can Move On	72
5	Goals? You Bet! Goals Make Us Who We Are	94
6	Courage is to Start; The Rest Will Come	98
7	Be Kind!	104
8	The Aha! Moment	106
	Studies for Success	111
	About the Author	114

Chapter One

THE IMPORTANCE OF DECIDING WHAT YOU WANT

How many times have you felt like you were just gliding through life, accepting whatever came your way? When that happens, you feel like you have no control of your decisions, surroundings, or outcomes. You feel like you have no control of your life.

This has happened to many of us, and we get to that point because we don't think we are smart enough or have enough money to get what we want in life. We feel that we're simply walking through a life that was preplanned for us, one where we have no control, voice, or ability to change any aspect of it. It's like the life we're living is dictated to us, and we don't know how to change it, or if we ever really can.

The loss of control that results is one of the main reasons depression runs rampant in America. Depression often stems from disappointment, discouragement, unhappiness, or loss of control. The inability to make a decision, even a small one, causes a sense of hopelessness. However, when depression seeps in, it is important to make a decision. It can be as small as deciding to get a new hairstyle, taking a walk, or trying a new recipe. It doesn't have to be big, but it does have to be new and different. This small act will reveal that you do have the opportunity to impact your own life, and it will remind you that you don't have to accept the status quo. You will be surprised at the sense of control you will feel from making just one small decision.

The sense of hopelessness and lack of control over life affects everyone, and I am not an exception. I had three small children and found myself in a very bad and volatile marriage. Because I was young, I had no idea how to get out of the unhappy and unhealthy situation. I felt like I had absolutely no control over my future and feeling stuck, I desperately wanted to escape. Naturally, I became depressed. But rather than accepting this as my fate, I decided to do something—anything. I needed a reprieve, and it was increasingly important that I regain some control over my life. So, I decided to take my kids on a little trip once a week. The state border was only an hour and a half from our house, so I'd make snacks and drive my children across the state line to a park, where the kids could eat and play for an hour. It was a short trip, but it made all of us feel like we were getting away. More important, this small decision kept me sane for several years. It instilled a sense of control—you feel like you can do something, no matter how small, to make a difference in your life. This ability to control strengthens life and strengthens your confidence and gives you hope that you can get out of unhappy situations.

While gaining control over my life, I also learned something very important. Deciding what you want in life gives you control. You cannot work toward your future until you know what it is you want to be, have, or do in your future. For some people, this is difficult to determine. They simply don't know what they want. If that is the case, ask yourself the question in different ways. For instance, if you ask a room full of people to close their eyes and think of three things they really want or three things they want to change in their lives, they can do it. It is much easier to answer that specific question than it is to answer the broader question, "What do I want in my future?"

Knowing what you want is your roadmap to getting it. If you decide to drive to Florida for vacation, you have a road map, a GPS, that tells you the roads to take that will get you to your destination. But if you just say, "I'm going on a vacation," but don't know where you are going to go, it makes it quite difficult to pull out a road map and determine the route you need to take. You cannot get somewhere if you don't know where you want to go. It is also true that you cannot get the result you want in your life if you don't know what you want.

Maybe you want a better job or a promotion at work. You might dream of owning your own business, achieving wealth, finding success that involves a passion or hobby, or maybe you want a better marriage. You might want to find a new relationship or improve your relationship with family members. Some people want a larger home or new friends. Somewhere within you, there is something that you want. However, within you is also an inner core that closes you off from what you want, thinking, no, it's never going to happen. If you really open it up, though, you will find it holds the key to what you really want in life.

Sometimes we are just scared to say what we want. We are afraid to recognize or acknowledge it because we think we can't have it. In that case, we are protecting ourselves from possible (or in our minds, probable) disappointment. But if we don't recognize what we want, we can't possibly ever have it. It would be like winning the lottery without ever buying a ticket. It's just not going to happen.

Deciding what it is that you want is the first and most important step. You will develop a newfound confidence just by knowing what you want and then you can take steps to get it. It's the starting point of your road map, and once that's determined, you can get there one mile, one turn, and one road at a time. Keep travelling toward your destination, and you will eventually get there.

It's amazing that once you know what you want, you will start seeing the opportunities that surround you. I know we all hear the word "opportunity" a lot. We're told to find our opportunities and take advantage of our opportunities, but do we really know what opportunity looks like? Too often, we do not, but we will talk about that later in the book.

First, you need to know what the vision of what you want looks like. I'm going to tell you about the first time I really knew what I wanted in life. When I stated what my vision was and what I wanted in life, everything changed for me. It happened when my father died very early in life from lung cancer. He was 58 years old. My parents had never been very good with finances and lived from pay day to pay day and sometimes relied on credit cards. My dad had a business, but it was always a balancing act between playing catch up and paying taxes. They were still relatively young and trying to keep the business afloat. Understandably, when my dad passed away, they were not prepared. There was not much life insurance, only enough to pay his burial expenses. My mother had to give up her home and didn't have the funds to take care of herself. My sister and I had to help her financially every month. My mother hated this and became resentful and bitter. I knew right then that this was not what I wanted for my life. I told myself, *I don't know how yet, but I will make sure I make a good living to always care for myself and not have to depend on family members or friends.*

Yes, my father's death was a tragedy for me and my family. I was a daddy's girl and took his death very hard, BUT this was the first time I really knew what I wanted in the future. As time went on, I found other visions for my future, but this was the first definite vision I had.

At the time of my father's death, I was managing a print shop. I made the decision then that I would open my own printing company. I saw it as an opportunity that would bring me closer to my vision. Because I had never owned a business before, I spent a year learning what I would need to know as an owner. I studied how to make a business plan and how to find the equipment and the lease space. I put together a plan with the costs for opening the business. I went to a small business seminar that gave me great tips on starting a business. To fund the business, I decided to get a minority women's bank loan. When I went to apply for a small business loan, I was told I had to apply at two regular banks for the loan, and when they both turned me down, I could come back for the minority small business loan. Well, when I went to the first bank and gave them my business plan, they were taken back and said it was one of the most thorough business plans they had seen. They gave me the loan, and I was on my way. I was on the first road to my destination.

> *"Knowing what you want is the true battle."*

Excitement in Your Everyday Life

Once you have decided what you want in life, that's when the fun can begin. It's very exciting to know what you want. For one reason, you'll be one of a very few who know what they want. It also reduces so much stress from your life. Instead of feeling hopeless or uncertain, you know what you want and what you're going to do! Now all you must do is have fun and look for the opportunities that will get you what you want. From that point on, you will constantly be looking at everything and every situation in your life completely differently. It is like putting on vision glasses and suddenly seeing things that you couldn't see before.

Something else happens when you know what you want in life. For the first time, when things happen in your life, you see them as opportunities. Whatever comes your way, you will look at it and ask, "How can this situation help me get to where I want to be?" This is true even when the situation isn't cause for celebration.

Many years back, a fire burned my home to the ground. It was a rough and stressful time; I lost many personal things that couldn't be replaced. Anything that could be replaced had to be, and that meant all of my furnishings, appliances, and personal belongings. Now, I love to shop and consider myself somewhat of a pro at shopping, but when you have nothing and walk into a department store, it is overwhelming. I didn't know what to do first. It's certainly wasn't fun, like shopping for enjoyment can be. But I found there was a silver lining—the loss of my house actually presented me with an opportunity. I had to rebuild the house, and I was able to do remodel and make it much more valuable when I was ready to sell it later. I did sell the home two years later and was able to get 20 percent more than the asking price. That was very exciting!

Every day, you will be looking for opportunities that will further your goal to succeed. It gives you a step up and makes you feel like you know something others don't. Here's a secret: that's not just a feeling—it is true. Others don't know what you know because most people go through life unsure of what they want or afraid to go for it.

Once I opened my print shop, I was ecstatic and so proud of myself! It was also terrifying to know that I had a loan to pay back every month. I knew this was the beginning of reaching what I wanted, to be financially independent of anyone. However, the business wasn't all about money. It was a fun business and a family business. My kids got involved and often helped. I had a customer who had us print a community newsletter every month. Once it was printed, I took it home and, that evening, I put a movie on that the kids would like and made popcorn. I passed out parts of the newsletter to each kid, and we passed it around and collated the pages to complete the newsletter. It was fun for the kids and served the purpose of preparing the newspaper.

About that time, my daughter was in the second grade. She went to school one day and saw her teaching collating papers. She approached her teacher and asked if she could help. The teacher asked me how my daughter knew what collating meant at her age. I laughed and explained to her that we collated a newsletter every month. This was exciting for me and my kids. It was an opportunity for me to teach my children how to do something new, and they felt like they were contributing to the success of my print shop.

It's fun to include your family and find interesting ways for them to help you with your journey. Involving my children made the process more exciting and fulfilling. Share your dreams with your family and let them be a part of your success. Sometimes we tend to move on our dreams alone and leave behind others who don't understand what we are doing. This can make them resentful and as is they're left out, when being included can be so much more rewarding for everyone.

"Don't feel bad for making decisions that upset others. You're not responsible for their happiness; you're responsible for yours."

Confidence

When you have a goal and commit to it, there is a sense of reassurance that you are headed in the right direction. Imagine setting out to go somewhere, without a clue where you're going. You wander aimlessly, sometimes in circles, hoping you're getting closer, instead of farther, from where you want to be. In this case, every step you take is uncertain. Am I doing the right thing or the wrong thing? Should I be veering to the left or to the right. Of course, it's not difficult to imagine that you aren't taking this journey with any sense of confidence. Confidence only comes with reasonable certainty that you're doing the right thing in the right way.

Knowing what you want in life and going after it will bring you a very confident feeling. You will have a feeling of purpose in everything you do. It will bring you clarity in the decisions you make. Yes, you will have trials and road bumps, but perseverance will overcome because you are confident in what you want and unwavering in your desire to make it happen.

When I started my printing company, I had to hire employees to help run the company. One day, when I had only been open a couple months, one of my employees came in on a Monday morning, and she was so excited. She said, "Look outside in the parking lot, see that brand-new truck out there? My husband and I bought it this weekend." She was beaming from ear to ear. She was so thrilled over that truck.

I looked at the truck and the great big smile on her face, and it struck me like lightening! I had a responsibility to these employees to be successful with this business. It wasn't just my livelihood that was in jeopardy, but my employees' livelihoods were also at stake. This realization hit me like a ton of bricks. I ran to the bathroom and actually got sick from the realization that other families were relying on me. I felt like I had just bought that truck myself. But I learned something—I had so much confidence that I could run that business and that it would lead me to reaching what I wanted, that my employees could feel the confidence. They felt secure in their jobs and future. You realize that sometimes when you're building your life and trying to reach your goals, you're also taking other people along with you, and you must be responsible for those people.

At times, you will have doubts about whether about can actually get what you want. Sometimes, what you want might change. That's okay; life is always evolving and changing. But here is a word of caution: Even when you have doubts, you must be confident on the outside. You must always convey confidence in whatever you do. You must stay positive and solve whatever problem presents itself. Problem solving is what makes most people successful. In fact, problem solving is seen as an opportunity to successful people. That's because most people can't think out of the box or find solutions for problems.

Today, I am a real estate investor, and I know that problem solving is what makes real estate investors successful. The properties that have many problems are the ones you want to invest in. Because not everyone is capable of problem solving, there are fewer potential or competing buyers for these properties. Therefore, you can buy the property much cheaper and correct the problems, then sell it for more money and get a wider profit margin than someone who can't problem solve.

Don't let problems or roadblocks stop you from your dreams and desires. Stay confident that you can get over the roadblocks or find a way through the problems. There will always be something in the way. Success is sweet, but it doesn't come easy. It will come, though, if you persevere and stay confident that you can overcome obstacles.

"Nothing is impossible,
the word itself says,
"I'm possible."

Audrey Hepburn

Constant Learning

Once you know what you want, you must be willing to learn and seek the wisdom to accomplish it. Don't be scared to go after what you want because you don't know how to obtain it. When I opened my print shop, I had never owned a business. When I say I didn't know anything about being an entrepreneur, I'm not exaggerating. But I spent a year going to small business seminars and studied how to put a business plan together. You can educate yourself. It may take several steps and processes to get where you want to be. If you find yourself in a holding pattern, there are still things you can do to be ready for the day when that opportunity knocks at the door. First, believe in what you want and start educating yourself. Read books on the subject and find people who have been successful in the same business or industry. See how they did it. Go to seminars and conferences that can provide you with the information and knowledge you'll need. Learn what you don't know and become a master at your trade.

Most successful people have failed once or twice, but they didn't give up. That's the difference between successful people and unsuccessful people. Successful people study what they did and figure out where they made a mistake, and then they take steps to correct it and try again. Unsuccessful people usually blame their results on others or on situations. Because they are not accountable, willing to admit they made a mistake and learn from it, they never reach their dream or goal.

My ex-husband and I had a fireworks business together. We had large warehouses where we sold consumer fireworks to the public for the 4th of July and New Year holidays. Our company was the largest in two states. But when we started the company, we had a partner. He knew all about fireworks, and he ran the stores. Two days before we were to open for our July season, he died, and we had to take over the stores. We discovered that the stores were not ready to open in two days, and, unfortunately, we didn't know anything at all about ordering products. We did, however, know one person who knew quite a bit about fireworks. We called him, and he was able to help us place a product order and set up the stores in time for the season to open. We had a successful season, even though we had no clue what we were doing. The business is now extremely successful, and we made a point of making sure we understand it completely.

Seek out someone who does know what you need to learn and don't be scared to ask for help or advice. Don't give up because you're not an expert, just keep learning and trying. Go to every seminar and conference you can find, even if there is some repetition. Remember, you always get at least one thing from every seminar or conference you attend. You may only need to learn 10 percent of what they are teaching, but that's 10 percent more knowledge you will acquire that will help move you toward what you want. And don't forget another important benefit—each conference, seminar, and workshop will connect you with people you've never met before and who can perhaps help you or put you in contact with someone they know who can.

No matter how old we are, we can still learn something new every day. Make sure you learn everything you need to know for your dream. You may be very good at something, but if you want to make it a business, you might need to learn about running a business. Take every opportunity to learn about your business or passion. Don't be closed minded and think you have all the answers. We can always learn from others; we learn from both their mistakes and their successes. Most important, we learn from our own mistakes. Very few success stories are written without a couple unsuccessful chapters. But those chapters only serve to make us so much happier and more appreciative when success is achieved.

"We are allowed to make mistakes, but let's not allow our mistakes to make us."

Be a Role Model

Knowing what you want and going after it is something few people achieve. As you find opportunities around you in your everyday life, the people around you will be in awe. They will be shocked to find that you took a bad situation and turned it into an opportunity. Or they might be surprised to learn that you spend your time differently so you can reach your dreams. Instead of watching TV, you now read books that strengthen your knowledge and teach you. Instead of going to a ball game, you opt to go to a seminar. People will notice the change. What kind of role model do you think that would be for your kids, grandkids, and family? Your family may not understand why you are changing the way you live your life, but they will respect and look up to you for trying to accomplish your goals and dreams. Once you achieve the dream or goal, they will look to you as an example and will want you to mentor them.

But be aware that there will be family and friends who see your success and say things like, "I want to be you." The truth is that they usually don't want to be you. They want your success, but they don't want to invest the hard work that it took for you to get there. Most people are not willing to sacrifice and work hard to obtain their dreams. That's one of the biggest deterrents to success there is. It's easy to make the mistake of being flattered when friends say they wanted to be like you. You will find yourself voluntarily taking them on and trying to help them find their passion and dream. You may even invest money in them and their dream, and after six months or so, you see that they didn't want to do the work it takes to be successful. That's unfortunate, but it's just part of the school of hard knocks. Experience is an excellent instructor. You have to learn that not everyone is cut out for the hard work that success requires. That hard work is what sets you apart from the rest.

It's a consistent never give up, never quit mentality. You are willing to do what it takes to get there. You find the opportunities that will bring you a step forward, and sometimes those opportunities present themselves in times of tragedy or misfortune. My decision and opportunity came when my father died. But there are other times when you might only see sadness, fear, or uncertainty. Have you ever heard the saying, "Sometimes, not getting what you want is a blessing." Losing a job seems devastating, but it creates new opportunities. Divorce might seem to be devastating, but it puts you in a position where you can have a fresh start—one where you are in total control of your future.

When you make a decision and really know what you want, opportunities will come. Attending the SBA seminar was a great opportunity for me. Having a friend who was a very excellent printer and wanted to change jobs was a great opportunity for starting a business. It was also nice to sell the business three years later for a profit.

I had friends in real estate who wanted me to work with them. I agreed and took the classes I needed to obtain my real estate license. I partnered with my friend, and we hit upon another opportunity. We lived on one side of town, and people were moving into our city every day. However, most of them wanted to live on the other side of town. All the other agents in our office said there was no way they were driving all the way across town to show property, so my partner and I said we would love to take the relocations. We put families in our cars and drove across town to show them properties. In doing this, we found out that nine out of ten families wanted a new home, not a resale. So, we started taking them to home builders and signing them up. The home builders would take care of everything, the contract, build, and closing. As realtors, the only thing we did was take them to the home builder's properties. When they closed, we would get a big commission check in the mail. It was gravy money, but the other agents could only see that it took 35 minutes to go across town. It was a great opportunity, and my partner and I took advantage of it. We made a ton of money on relocations. The other agents thought we were brilliant and looked at us as role models, but all we did was take advantage of an opportunity that they couldn't see.

You will be a role model to many but be careful because there is no shortage of people who want to ride on your shirttails, instead of doing the work themselves. You can mentor them on to their journey to find what they want, but they must do the work themselves.

> *"If your actions create a legacy that inspires others to dream more, learn more, do more and become more, then you're an excellent leader."*
>
> *Dolly Parton*

Recognizing the Opportunities

Opportunities lead you to your success, and they are everywhere. They live in your daily life. Doing something no one else wants to do, like driving across town to sell homes, was a huge opportunity. But it was there for other people, too—they just couldn't see it, even though it was right before their eyes! They'd even been asked to partake in the opportunity and turned it down. That's because they saw it as a waste of time, rather than an opportunity. Most people don't recognize opportunities that are right in front of them because they are blinded by what they may or may not be willing to do. But trust me, opportunity is there, often staring at your face, tapping on your door. Some people just can't see it for what it is, even when it's so obvious that if it was a snake, it would have bit them!

The majority of people wouldn't buy the residential homes we bought over the years, because they needed work or had a problem they don't know how to fix. These are not problems to me; they are opportunities. I look at such "problems" and ask, *How can this benefit me? How can I use this to my advantage?* The home's problems are an opportunity to buy the property much cheaper. You can then make the repairs and solve the problem and sell the home and have a wider profit margin than most. Being a problem solver is great for taking advantage of opportunities.

When I was involved in owning the fireworks business, the inventory was stored in the warehouse all year. However, we were only open 21 days a year. It seemed like a waste to have that space sit idly for more than 300 days every year, but we couldn't rent out the warehouse because we needed it during those 21 days. So, I saw an opportunity! I noticed that temporary Halloween stores were popping up in empty storefronts all over town. So, I decided I could do the same with our fireworks warehouses. What a great opportunity! So, before Halloween we would move the inventory out of the warehouse and put in Halloween inventory. We had an advantage over the other temporary stores because we were at the same spot every year, while the other stores had to move around to available empty spots. We built up a great Halloween business, which became the largest in our city with several stores every year.

Sometimes problem solving and opportunities are the same thing. An opportunity is just the vessel to make something happen. You see, sometimes opportunities aren't just lying in the bushes waiting for you to find them. Sometimes, you make the opportunity. They are seeds that have to planted, nurtured, and harvested. Opportunities are decisions you make and problems you solve. They can be things that no one else wants to do or reactions to adversity that come your way. Opportunity is stepping out of your usual and making something happen. Don't wait for it to show up at your door, because it will never come knocking.

Too often, when we're stuck in a place where we don't want to be, we cannot see a path out. Unemployed, we don't have any luck finding a job. Single and lonely, it seems that all of the good ones are already taken. When the bank account is empty or doesn't exist, it can be difficult to imagine a day when money isn't your greatest challenge. At some time, we are challenged with these and other problems. When that happens, it is difficult to be optimistic and envision that anything will change.

But it can … and it will—if you make your own opportunities.

The ways to create your own opportunities are countless, limited only by your creativity. That said, I found a few that are not only impressive, but sometimes also quite entertaining. Read along and you just might find yourself saying, "Why didn't I think of that?!"

1. Unemployed, Kelly Kinney printed her resume on an unlikely place—a t-shirt! She wore it everywhere and found that people would stop her so they could finish reading it. What a great way to get noticed and stand out in a crowd. As a bonus, potential employers would be impressed by your creativity and ingenuity.

2. Let your car be a "job wanted" ad. For the low cost of printing a bumper sticker, you can have everyone else on the highways and byways help you find work. It's as easy as printing: Reward if you get me a job: BobtheSalesman.com.

3. Make your signature line an advertisement for what you want. Everyone who reads your emails, text messages, and even social media posts will see it. You never know what the exposure will bring your way.

4. Reignite your business cards. Pull out your old business cards, or get some new ones, and pass them out to people you see. Sitting at Starbucks? Stop by a table, say hello, and hand them a

business card with a simple offer to "let me know if I can help you."

Don't know how to get creative? Write down your situation (out of work, underemployed, financially unstable, single and hatin' it, etc.), then list ways you can turn this into a positive. What unique opportunities are there in this situation? And better yet, what can you do differently today to seize those opportunities? Remember, taking the first step is akin to planting a seed that could sprout and grow, bringing you an abundance of what you want.

Every day, we have opportunities. We have an opportunity to be productive or lazy. We have an opportunity to be optimistic or pessimistic. We have an opportunity to help or hinder. We have an opportunity to give up or step up and go get what we want. We have an opportunity to bemoan our circumstances or do something to change them. There is always an opportunity to do one thing, to take one step toward our dreams. There are opportunities that are readily visible, and opportunities that are harder to identify, especially during emotional times. But rest assured, opportunities are there, whether they are screaming or silent.

Actress Charlize Theron found opportunity in a very strange place, and it did involve screaming. Standing in line at a Los Angeles bank, she was attempting to cash an international check from her mother in South Africa. However, the bank refused to cash it. This did not make Charlize happy, and she was quite vocal about it. Yelling at the teller, she threw what could be defined as an adult temper tantrum. Some say it was of epic proportions. Now, for most, this wouldn't get us anywhere, but an agent was also in line and witnessed what he called her passionate performance, and opportunity was born.

While I don't condone throwing a fit in public as a way to get noticed and attract opportunities, Charlize's experience shows us that opportunity is everywhere. It's in the coffee shop, a business event, and even in line at the bank. Sometimes, it just needs you to *do something* in order for it to present itself.

What do you want? A new car? Your first home or a larger one? Your own business? To be financially independent, even wealthy? To be fit and healthy? Maybe you want multiple streams of income or a fulfilling relationship. Whatever you want, I assure you that it is possible—if you're willing to put in the work for the reward, and if you are able to recognize the opportunities before you.

They're there. Find them.

"Only those who have the habit of going the Extra Mile, ever find the end of the rainbow."

Napoleon Hill

Chapter Two

WHAT KEEPS US FROM GETTING WHAT WE WANT

Let's admit it, at one time or another, most of us have looked around at the people around us and wondered why and how they get what they want, but we never seem to be able to get what we want. We sigh, thinking they're the luckiest people alive. If it's gloomy outside, we feel like we're under a dark storm cloud, while it seems to be raining rainbows over them. They get promotions on a regular basis, and they're recognized and rewarded at every turn. In short, everything seems so easy for them, while everything seems to be such a struggle for the rest of the world.

What do they know that we don't know? Is it luck, or is there something more?

Getting what you want doesn't have anything to do with four-leaf clovers, rabbit feet, or "good luck." Getting what you want is not outside of your control. The good news is that you have a great deal of power and control over your circumstances and your life. The problem is that you don't know what's holding you back from getting what you want. In this chapter, we will uncover the underlying issues that keep what you want in life at bay.

Fear of Failure and Fear of the Unknown

We tend to be scared of the unknown. Sometimes, it's easier to deal with what we know—even if it's not something we really want. That's because we have an internal fear that any change could actually be worse, not better.

For example, we might prefer to stay in an unhappy marriage or in a dead-end job because we fear that we'll never find another relationship or may end up in a job that makes us even more miserable. I was in an abusive marriage, and I'm proof that women will stay in an abusive marriage because living with the abuse actually seems easier than the unknowns of leaving.

Not knowing what the future holds, we lack the confidence to make major changes in our lives. Frankly, we need reassurance that we are, indeed, doing the right thing. Until we get it, status quo is where we'll remain.

My first marriage was unhappy, but I was even more scared of the fact that I wouldn't be able to support and care for three children by myself than I was of the abuse. I knew I was able to do whatever it took to take care of my family, but I was truly scared of the unknown—what would my life be like? What if it would be even worse?

The same is true for jobs. Even though we spend more than one-third of our days at our workplace, approximately 70 percent of employees are unhappy with their job or their career. Yet, they are afraid to make a major change, staying in a miserable job because they are scared to look for another job. What if no one wants to hire them? What if another job isn't any better ... what if it is worse?

A good friend who worked for a bank for many years constantly complained about how much they took advantage of her. They would use her to get loans because she was very good with people. She could sell ice to an Eskimo, and she helped all of the loan officers acquire loans and make money. Even more, she helped them go above and beyond the quotas set by their company. She never received anything for her major contribution and skill; there was no monetary raise or bonus or even an acknowledgement of her contribution to their success.

Naturally, she was quite unhappy. She felt unappreciated to the point where she would get furious and say she wasn't going to do their jobs anymore, but the next week, she'd be back at her desk, back at it again, making sure they kept getting the same results she'd always brought to them. Why? First, she was a natural—she was good at what she did. Second, she loved what she did—she just didn't love the company she worked for and how she was being treated. People would constantly tell her that with her talents and record, she could easily get another job, but she wouldn't even attempt to apply for another job. She was afraid of the unknown and the possibility of rejection, which she feared, even more than being used by the lazy banking staff.

Realistically, though, what is the worst thing that can happen? You apply for a job and don't get an offer? Yes, you might feel rejected. But this will happen to you, not once, not twice, but many times if you want to go after your dreams and desires. It's part and parcel of success. There will be times that you don't get the job or find that things don't work out the way you really wished they would have. But you must let it roll off your back and keep believing in yourself. No one else is going to believe in you unless you believe in yourself. Here's a critical point: if you want to get what you want, you cannot do it without confidence and belief in yourself.

If you know what it is you want and you're confident that you are going to obtain it, even if it doesn't happen instantly, then rejection or naysayers won't matter to you at all. You know where you are headed, and you have to keep your eyes open, looking forward for the opportunities that will come your way now that you know what you want. They will as long as you remain confident and don't give up.

The list of people who failed after rejection and failure is seemingly endless. Here are a few:

Thomas Edison: The world might still be dark if Edison had given up after failing to create the light bulb a whopping 1,000 times!

Theodor Seuss Giesel: Even though his first book was rejected 27 times, he didn't give up. Today, children across the world enjoy 47 beloved books by the whimsical, lyrical writer, Dr. Seuss.

Charles Schultz: The famous Peanuts creator and illustrator was once rejected by Disney!

Walt Disney: Only 22 years old, Walt Disney was fired by a newspaper, ironically, for not being creative enough. He went on to win 32 Academy Awards and still holds the record for the most Oscars won by an individual. And I beg anyone to question his creativity today—the results speak for themselves.

Stephen King: King threw his manuscript, Carrie, into the trash after receiving 30 rejections. In this case, his wife believed in him more than he believed in himself. Carrie was published and later became an iconic thriller on the big screen. Since then, Stephen King has published hundreds of books and is known as one of the world's bestselling authors.

Babe Ruth: The legendary homerun record holder, Babe Ruth also held another record—the record for most strikeouts (1,330 total). Being the worst isn't a record anyone wants, but it was because of his failures that he was so great. According to Babe, "Every strike brings me closer to my next homerun."

Michael Jordan: Quite possibly one of the best players to play professional basketball, Michael Jordan didn't make the cut for his high school team. That rejection made him try even harder. Even after he gained incredible success, he points out his failures: "I have missed more than 9,000 shots in my career. I have lost almost 300 games. On 26 occasions I have been entrusted to take the game winning shot, and I missed. I have failed over and over and over again in my life. And that is why I succeed."

It is that attitude that made children everywhere say that they want to be like Mike. Shouldn't we all want to be more like Mike and use our failures, rejections, and setbacks as fuel to prove the naysayers wrong ... and prove ourselves right?

> *"If you hear a voice within you say you can't paint, then by all means paint, and that voice will be silenced."*
>
> Vincent Van Gogh

Peer Pressure

Sometimes you will find that you are your own greatest critic and enemy. At other times, you are surprised to find that the people who are closest to you are the very ones who don't have your back. As you're on your journey toward success, you will have many friends and family who do not understand this quest. They know you as you are and as you've always been. They're used to you and like you just the way you are. Suddenly, as you make changes to pursue your dream, they feel slighted or left out. Silently, they might be a little jealous, or they may be openly critical.

Here's a typical scenario. Let's say you've always gone to the ballgame with your friends, or maybe you've barbequed with your family every Saturday. But suddenly you decline the invitations—maybe you have an opportunity to grow and learn at a seminar or conference.

Maybe you're going back to school or have committed to take more time to read professional or personal growth books. Maybe you're trying to save money, so you don't want to go to the ballgame every weekend, which would save you a couple hundred dollars a month.

Here's the bad news: Your friends and family members usually won't understand why you've changed. They will feel cheated, like you're moving on and leaving them behind. Maybe they'll think that your dreams are more important to you than they are. There is a good reason they won't understand your motives—most of them will not even be able to tell you what it is *they* want most in life. The fact that you know what you want might even be threatening to them.

Why is that? Any change or shift in the status quo can cause feelings of unease. They might have the misdirected feeling that you think you are better than them or that you don't like them anymore. Perhaps, they might believe that you're outgrowing them (and perhaps that is true). We get comfortable with routines, and when that routine changes, it stirs emotions. Your friends and family might feel slighted by you, even disposable in your life. And they will push back to avoid that happening.

Without being intentional, they will be jealous and may make fun of your new goals in life. Unfortunately, they might even become your biggest naysayers, telling you there is no way you can achieve your goals or dreams. They will give you reason after reason that it won't work. They don't do this because they want you to be unhappy, but they do it because they feel threatened … they don't want to be unhappy … and the fact that you are impacting their comfortable routine makes them fear the unknown.

Yes, it's possible that they might even try to discourage you from pursuing your goals because they don't want you to fail. They don't want you to get hurt. They simply cannot understand that there is even a remote possibility that you might succeed, because they don't know the secret that you now have found—that now that you know what it is that you want, the opportunities will be recognizable to you.

You must be around supportive people and family. If so, great—count yourself fortunate. If you are around negativity, however, it will bring you down. You will pick up on the negative vibes, and they will have an effect on your progress. You must surround yourself with people who are supportive and want the best for you. If you don't have positive, supporting people to talk to and share your dreams with, you will feel very isolated and it will be so much harder to stay on course.

While you cannot change your family, you can choose who you want to spend the majority of your time with. You might have to limit the time you spend with family members who don't support you on your mission. You might have to give up relationships with people who have been your friends for many years. You don't have to turn your back on them and write them out of your life, but if you want to succeed, you will want to spend less time with them. It won't take long before you realize that you don't have as much in common as you used to — your horizons are broadening while theirs are not. Because they invoke negativity or a bad attitude into your journey, you'll find that you don't want to talk about your journey for success with them.

However, you will find that you do love talking to others who are on their own quest or who have already achieved success and walked in the steps you are taking now. They will be a source of encouragement and support, and they will inject you with the inspiration and motivation to achieve whatever you want.

People who have already accomplished what you want will lift you up, while others may put you down. Those who have accomplished what you want will also give you some much-needed advice and help push you through the obstacles and challenges that may present themselves. Experience is a great teacher and mentor, and they will help you and be your cheerleaders as you pursue your goals.

Now that doesn't mean that your family is to blame. After all, they think they've known you all your life, and they think that puts them in a position to know what's best for you. The problem is, they see you as the person you might have been years ago, but now you've changed. You've grown, and your goals and aspirations have changed and grown, as well. Remember the fear of the unknown? Well, they've loved you for as long as they've known you. Maybe they're afraid that they're not going to love the new successful you … or that the new successful you won't love them in the same way, either.

Sometimes your family can't recognize your successes. They can get stuck in the past and who you were as a young child or adult. This can be hurtful when you have worked hard to gain your success, but you have to put it aside and be happy for your success, even if they're not on board. This is where the friends you choose are valuable. They will lift you up and celebrate with you.

 Post some of your accomplishments and special events on social media, and thankfully, you will have tons of friends who respond positively—people who are encouraging and happy for you. However, you may not receive a single response from family members. While you don't want to separate yourself from your family, you may need to learn to separate them from your success. It's the only way you can keep your eye on the prize—because if you use your energy, time, and effort to try to win their approval, it will require that you shift your focus. You know you cannot change them, so choose to focus on what you can do.

"Look who your people are that are always there for you, that want better for you, they are your people."

Looking Backward

Oh, hindsight—that animal that we can't keep down and keeps raising its ugly head. We spend a lot of time punishing ourselves for our past mistakes. We all have done things in our past that we regret or wish we hadn't done. Heck, we've all made mistakes. It's part of life. However, it doesn't have to haunt us forever. Yet we don't forgive ourselves and keep looking back at the shadow of regret, instead of forward toward the light of success.

Why do we do this? Mistakes are painful, and they impact our self-esteem. When we live with regret or past mistakes, we don't believe we deserve the success or rewards that we are looking to obtain. That's unfortunate because these mistakes can put us in a prison of misery for a lifetime, or until we let them go and forgive ourselves.

To move forward with your quest, you must forgive yourself for your past and whatever things you may have done that you're not proud of. The past is the past. You can't go back and change it, rewriting the chapter so the ending comes out the way you wished it had. So, stop beating yourself up over it. Haven't you punished yourself long enough?

I spent a good part of my life in an abusive marriage, feeling that I didn't deserve anything more. But that's in my past. Sure, I recognize that my marriage wasn't great, and it wasn't the best decision I ever made. But I forgive myself, especially for staying in the marriage as long as I did. Forgive yourself for the bad decisions you may have made. Forgive yourself for any failures. Those things are what made you who you are today. They were learning experiences. They gave you new insight. They strengthened your resolve. They served as your motivation for something better and more fulfilling. If you didn't have that experience, you wouldn't be the person you are today. You wouldn't have chosen the path that you took or been able to see the opportunities that came your way.

You have to make the decision that you are WORTH the success you want in life. You deserve all the success you can accomplish. Once I realized that I was a good person, mother, wife, friend, and daughter, I was able to let go of the past and move forward. I was able to get out of the bad marriage and start working toward my goals. I found out I was very strong and able to continue to grow and become a better person. One by one, I accomplished my goals, even though it wasn't always easy. My goals have changed many times over the years and yours will, too. It evolves with your life and how your life progresses over the years.

Today is the first day of the rest of your life. Heard that before? Don't let your past hold you back. Come to terms with the past and leave it there. Today is a brand-new day, and it's a good day for a very good day. Every day is the first day of the rest of your life. But if you keep living with shame or regret over your past, every day will be just like yesterday. Do yourself a favor and leave the past where it belongs, behind you. It has no place inside you anymore. The only thing you can control is today and your future. If the past didn't serve you well, don't let it rob you of your future, too.

And let's not forget that in our unfortunate past, there may lie an opportunity. This was true for actor Mel Gibson. One day, his friend asked him for a ride to an audition. Gibson obliged, even though he had gotten into a drunken fight the night before that left his face a little worse for the wear. It was his bruises and scrapes that caught the director's notice, and Gibson was offered a part as a villain in a movie—all because he looked the part. Once he healed, leading roles came his way. But he would have never gotten his break, and lucrative career, if it hadn't been for a night that most of us would have wished never happened.

"The past cannot be changed. The future is yet in your power."

Laziness

Reaching your goals or dreams is a process. It takes energy and focus. As they say, it is a marathon, not a sprint. It is reached step by step, milestone by milestone. Just as it is in any marathon (or sprint), you won't get anywhere if you don't get moving. You cannot achieve your dreams by sitting on the couch and watching TV. If you want financial security or wealth, sitting in the house, waiting for Publisher's Clearinghouse to knock on the door isn't going to make it happen. For most of us, neither will buying a lottery ticket. Opportunity doesn't come to you—you have to go out and find it.

There are two major obstacles to success, and they are procrastination and laziness. Don't get lazy. Light a fire under your dreams. Light a fire under your legs and in your mind. Take action, even if it is just one little step every day, toward your goal. Remember Newton's first law? An object in action will remain in action. An object at rest will remain at rest. If you do nothing, you'll get nowhere. If you do something, you will make progress toward your goals. No matter how small that progress is, you'll be closer than you were yesterday.

You have to make active choices to move toward your goals. No one else can make it happen for you. It's up to you to find the opportunities you need to reach your goals and success. Once you know what you want, you must have your Opportunity glasses on all the time. You must be aware of situations that come your way and turn them into opportunities.

Any situation that comes up in your life needs to be evaluated so you can determine how it can be turned into an opportunity that will move you toward your goals. This is true for even negative situations. Maybe your company is downsizing—that could open up new opportunities for you. Maybe your marriage is over—somewhere in that situation lies an opportunity that you haven't yet considered. Opportunities are all around you, and not only in life-changing situations. Every day, there are things that happen, and you have to recognize the opportunity in them. They were presented to you with a label that says

Opportunity—you just failed to look closely enough to read that label.

Sometimes, we all get used to the norm. We drive to and from work every day and see the same things so often that we don't even pay attention to them anymore. The same is true in everything we do. We don't recognize and fail to see something that is right in front of our eyes because we've seen it so often that we've become blind to it. We've become mentally lazy.

Don't be lazy and ignore the things that are going on around you; they are your opportunities. You must take action to reach your goals. You must maintain a timeline to achieve your goals. If you don't, the outcome will be that you don't achieve your goals and success.

It takes work and attention to achieve your goals. No one is going to tell you to sit back, take a seat—they'll do it for you. No one is going to say, "Hey, don't worry—I've got this." If you think they will, you're going to wait a long, long time … and you're highly likely to be disappointed. The truth is that those who achieve their goals are those who never stop working toward them. They know it's a marathon, not a sprint, so they don't run out of gas and stop. They don't give up. They get behind the starting line and take one step after another, until one mile at a time, they feel the thrill of personal victory and receive the success they so deserve.

That success is waiting for you, too. Put your best ambition foot forward and go out and get it.

"If you want something, you can make it happen, so go for it."

Chapter Three

WHAT CAN WE DO TO MOVE TOWARD SUCCESS?

Oh, no! You made a mistake! What now? Don't panic—it's not the end of the world. In reality, a mistake is not the end-all that we perceive it to be. On the contrary, if we change our perspective, one mistake can be the turning point we've been looking for in your entire life or career.

When it comes to mistakes, we have a tendency to punish ourselves—to beat ourselves up—for making them. That's a mindset that others have taught us, and it has been ingrained into our minds as a negative. And it's no wonder. Make a mistake in your checkbook ledger and the bank punishes you by charging overdraft fees. Make a mistake on a test and you'll get a big red check mark next to it, leaving your paper looking like it's been slapped on its face. When we make mistakes at work or in relationships, we immediately feel guilty ... and fearful that it will create permanent, irreversible damage.

I propose that mistakes should be approached with an opposite mindset. For instance, what would happen—what *could* happen—if we didn't view mistakes as something to be ashamed of and, instead, chose to view them as a valuable experience, a learning lesson, or, say, an opportunity?

You see, the path to success isn't always smooth. The skies aren't always bright and sunny. Regardless, the path is still there—it doesn't change. We have a choice what to do on that path and how we respond to what happens while we're on it. A mistake can stall us, temporarily or permanently, if we let it. Or we can use that mistake as a learning tool that provides valuable education that helps us grow closer to success.

That is precisely what I propose you do—let your mistakes work for you, not against you. Here's how you can do just that.

No One is Perfect

In a perfect world, everything would go as planned. Everything we do would be nothing short of excellence, and we would never make mistakes. But there's just one insurmountable problem with that—our perfect world is imperfect. We are imperfect. Each and every one of us is human, and humans are on a lifelong learning expedition. Only by making mistakes can we learn the valuable lessons that will prevent us from making the same mistake in the future.

All of us make mistakes. (What a boring world it would be if we didn't!) The most successful people make plenty of mistakes. Thomas Edison failed thousands of times before he created the light bulb. However, he didn't call them failures. *"I have not failed. I've just found 10,000 ways that won't work,"* he said. Elvis Presley was told he couldn't sing—he even failed music classes. A member of the Grand Ole Opry heard him sing once and, thinking he was doing him a favor in the long run, told him to go back to truck driving. "You ain't got what it takes, son." Basketball legend Michael Jordan was cut from his high school basketball team because he was not good enough. In the NBA, he missed more shots than he made. And that is precisely why he says he was successful. *"I have missed more than 9,000 shots in my career. I have lost almost 300 games. On 26 occasions I have been entrusted to take the game-winning shot, and I missed. I have failed over and over and over again in my life. And that is why I succeed."*

Any successful person will tell you that mistakes are required in order to be successful. You will make many mistakes and, yes, even experience failure before you succeed. When mistakes happen, and they will, don't beat yourself up about them. There's nothing wrong or evil about making mistakes. It's what you learn and do with the mistakes that will set you apart from everyone else. It's how you respond to the mistake that will determine the outcome.

Most people don't want to recognize their mistakes or admit they made a mistake; many people think it makes them look weak. But making mistakes is the best way of learning. You cannot shove it under a rug so you don't have to face it ever again. And you shouldn't feel like you have to hide it from the rest of the world in order to avoid their ridicule or criticism. You must move your ego out of the way to understand and recognize the mistake before that mistake can benefit you.

How do you do that? Encourage yourself to view a mistake as a positive. Yes, you read that right. Sure, it will immediately have a negative impact on you, but in the long-term, it can be the key to your success. Then you need to dig deeper and discover what went wrong and why.

Look at the situation. What went wrong? Was it one mistake or a series of mistakes that caused it? Knowing what you know now, what should you have done differently? This takes self-reflection, but that is necessary so you can gain the wisdom and experience that comes from this mistake. Then, you'll be smarter and wiser, and the next time you're in a similar situation, you can avoid making that mistake altogether.

Mistakes are your best opportunities in life if you are willing to look at them, accept them, and make changes from them. Many times, the best successes come from past mistakes that are turned into an opportunity. This was true for Spencer Silver, who worked at 3M. Silver was charged with the responsibility for making a super strong adhesive. However, he accidentally created the opposite—a weak and non-permanent adhesive that he called Acrylate Copolymer Microspheres. It was a mistake, and Silver failed in his mission to create what he'd been asked for. Unfortunately, the folks at 3M didn't see a use for his adhesive, and it was deemed unusable. Yes, it looked like Silver's invention was a failure. Somewhere along the way, he'd made a mistake in the process of trying to invent a super strong adhesive.

But was it a mistake … or an opportunity? 3M didn't see the opportunity, but a pastor did. That pastor needed to mark Bible pages for his services, but everything he used didn't work. Bookmarks and pieces of paper tucked into the pages slipped or fell out completely. He knew Silver and had heard about the weak adhesive, though, and turning lemons into lemonade, he created what has become a household word—Post It Notes.

Now, that's turning a mistake into an opportunity!

Mistakes do provide us with opportunities, if we can open our eyes and find them. Too often, we're too busy focusing on the mistake part of the situation that we fail to see how it can be a good thing—even if the only good thing that comes out of it is the fact that the mistake is one we can learn from so we don't repeat it again.

There's an old saying that "doing the same thing over and over, and expecting a different outcome, is insanity." Yet, it is surprising how many people do exactly that. They want to lose weight or get fit, but they are comfortable in their routine and don't change it. Without change, the results will always be the same. People will continue to get the same results, have the same relationships, and the same lifestyle if they keep doing the same thing they've always done. Even more important, they will keep experiencing the same life lessons and keep making the same mistakes unless they do something different to produce different results.

A nice woman, named Sara, dreamed of being a successful makeup artist. In fact, she was extremely talented and had a clientele. However, every day, Sara overbooked her appointments. As a result, she ran late every day, and the later the day went on, the more behind she was. Of course, this was an inconvenience that frustrated her clients. As it became routine, she even lost a couple clients. Sara was devastated. She couldn't understand why her clients would leave, especially since she was the best makeup artist around. When it was explained to her that people have commitments and need their makeup done on time so they wouldn't be late to their events, Sara responded with a multitude of excuses for why she was late. As a solution, it was suggested she take one less client on her busy days so she could get to each client on time. She said she couldn't afford to have fewer clients and if people wanted her to do their makeup, they would have to be patient and wait. Because Sara was arrogant and refused to acknowledge or understand that she was making a mistake, it cost her several clients and her business suffered severely. Instead of recognizing that she was making a mistake and addressing it by correcting it, Sara chose to do the insane thing—she did the same thing over and over and over again, expecting somehow to get different results.

But sometimes, people do opt to do something different, and they get totally different results. This has never been truer than in the case of criminals who have turned their lives around and now use their stories to inspire others to lead a law-abiding life. Many ex-convicts are public speakers who speak at schools and prisons, showing inmates and students alike that while mistakes can be costly, even life-changing, they don't have to be permanent—that it's never too late to learn from your mistakes. Above all, they are role models who exemplify the fact that in every mistake, there is, indeed, an opportunity to change their lives for the better.

The first step to make that happen is to forgive yourself. Recognize that you are human. Aren't we all guilty of sweating the small stuff sometimes? Don't fall into the trap of giving the mistake more merit and importance in your life than it deserves to have. Fretting about it for longer than necessary or realistic will serve no good purpose. Remember, it is human to err, so forgive yourself. Forgive yourself for your mistakes, but don't turn a blind eye to them. They're there to tell you that you need to make changes. Make the necessary changes so you don't repeat the same mistakes. But don't forget to look for the opportunities along the way!

"Doing the same thing over and over and expecting a different result is insanity."

Hang Out with Positive and Supportive People

In life, we have a habit of allowing negativity in our lives, and once it's there, we don't ask it to leave. We all know someone who is negative, and oftentimes, it is someone close to us. Unfortunately, a lot of the time the most negative people in our lives are family members or good friends. They might be pessimists who bemoan their bad luck all the time. They shoot down every idea or suggestion because they only see the potential for something that might go wrong. They keep themselves in pessimist jail, letting their negativity be a barrier between them and anything that might make a positive change in their life.

Negative people don't have dreams. They don't understand our dreams and are sometimes jealous of those who do. Because they can only see things in a negative light, they don't support change or pursuits that might bring happiness. Negativity is certainly not inspirational or motivational, so these people naturally bring us down, dragging us down to dwell in their world of woe.

Unfortunately, the negative people in our lives can have a significant impact on our growth and success. When we express our dreams or desires, they aren't supportive. Instead, they discourage us from pursuing what we want. Immediately, they rattle off everything that can go wrong and tell us why we should scrap our dreams. It's too hard. It'll never happen. You'll never make it. You can't afford it. What if you fail? They tend to tell us why we can't reach our vision and suggest all kinds of roadblocks we may encounter. Sometimes it comes from a place of what they consider love, trying to protect us from pain or disappointment. Many times, especially with family, it's because they tend to still see us at a certain age in life and get stuck in that time period for years.

Sometimes people don't see the long hours you put in or the sacrifices you make to gain your success; they just see the end result. Over time, you will learn that this inability to recognize your success is because they have not obtained success. They don't understand your success or what it takes to gain the success.

You want to have positive people in your life and surround yourself with them as often as possible. You want the people around you to be your biggest cheerleaders—people who will encourage you and urge you to keep going when you need it the most. You've got this! You can do it! You're going to make it! And even more important, how can I help you achieve your goals or dreams? Find people who have motivate and inspire you and will use their megaphone to push you forward.

One way to do that is to spend time with other successful people who will build you up and be positive for you. Successful people know that there will be drawbacks, mistakes, and challenges—but they also know from experience that every one of those things can be overcome. They know where you're at because they've been there. They know what is possible and tend to see the glass as either half full or flowing over the brim!

The people you surround yourself with should want the same thing you do—to achieve a dream, achieve a goal, or make a vision a reality. It doesn't have to be the same dream or the same goal or vision, but they need to have the same attitude and outlook. You need to have a common mission with them, to pursue your dreams and goals and support each other along the way. You want to know that these people are out in the world talking you up and bragging about you, not out there talking negative about you every time you turn your back.

You need positive people to throw your ideas at and get their opinions. These people you surround yourself with should be smarter or more successful than yourself. You will learn from these kinds of people, and they will give you encouragement. Some people call them mentors—people who have already succeeded at what you want to do and are willing to share their experience and wisdom with you. Not only that, but they will serve as your motivational can-do coach, providing you with support and positive encouragement in your endeavors. These people will always try to build you up, while the negative Nancys in your life will bring you down.

Don't let negative Nancy in your life. If she's already there, don't let her hang around.

You don't need to run your family off or kiss your old friends goodbye, but when you do spend time with them, do yourself a favor—don't share your goals and visions. Don't tell them about your dreams and aspirations. Keep the conversation on other, safer subjects. Talk about family things if you're with family. You may not want to talk and share your successes with them. Many times, unfortunately, family will be jealous of your success.

"This is a vital moment and shows who I am in how I respond."

Put a Networking Posse Together

While we're on the subject of people, did you know that the people you meet can introduce you to opportunities you've never seen before? Even more, they can spur you toward success faster than you can ever do on your own. No one can become successful alone. I wholeheartedly believe that. We all need support and help. We need people who will share their experience and knowledge with us.

Whatever your vision is, find the experts in that area or industry and reach out to them. If you're a real estate investor, seek the most successful investor you can find. If you want to be a model or an artist, find successful models who can tell you how they got there and artists who have their work displayed in galleries across the nation. Ask them questions and ask them to share what they know with you. Then soak up everything that they share. Most successful folks like to share. Thankfully, they also like to see others reach their dreams and goals. Use their goodwill to your benefit. Study what they do. Inquire about their habits, their goals, and their wisdom. Ask them to tell you what works and what doesn't. Seek their advice and follow it. Don't be afraid to learn from the ones who have already done it. Trust me, they won't think they're better than you—most successful people want to help you be better.

For that reason, ask away! Ask them anything you don't know. Don't think your questions are stupid or your lack of knowledge will make you look dumb. Remember, at one time, they were where you are now. They remember how it feels not to have all the answers. But now they are the ones with the knowledge.

We all have knowledge, but we have different knowledge, and one is not better than the other. You might be an electrician and feel intimidated by an attorney because they know so much more than you do about law. But that attorney doesn't know one thing about wiring and voltage. It's just an exchange of knowledge. It's a difference in interests, talents, and skills. One isn't smarter or better than the other—it's just different knowledge. And that's a wonderful thing! It provides people with so many more opportunities in a range of professions and industries.

Regardless of your interests or skillsets, there is an opportunity waiting for you. Create a network of people you can turn to make that opportunity a reality and use them to build your knowledge bank.

I was managing a print shop when I decided I wanted to open my own printing company. I studied the owner of the print shop so I could learn and understand the ins and outs of owning a print shop. I went to small business seminars and business conferences. I built a network around me, someone who knew the printing business, and others who understand the concept of managing a business, and still yet others who understood the equipment I had in my shop. I built a team of supporters who were more experienced than I, and I learned from them. Believe me, without their experience and expertise, I would have made more than my fair share of mistakes, and I would never have become a successful business owner in that industry without them.

When I started my real estate investments, I had an awesome mentor, who was very smart in all aspects of real estate and everything that goes with it, like tax law, legal issues, insurance, and formulas for buying properties. I was green and knew nothing about those things. I asked questions and learned everything I could and took full advantage of having this mentor to teach me. But before that could happen, I had to allow myself to learn and find ways to be around these types of people to network with.

Whatever your dream is, there are ways you can find a network of people who have the knowledge you need and will share it with you. You should search for groups or associations that involve your industry. Join them, attend their meetings. Go to their special events and explain to the people in the room what you're trying to do. Find out what their expertise is and what their strengths are. You'll gain something just by associating with them. Be around success and you will start thinking success—success is contagious, and it rubs off onto other people with like minds. On the other hand, hang around people who blame everyone else for their shortcomings, and you will find yourself doing the same thing. Remember, you want to be around people who motivate, inspire, and educate you—people who have no ulterior motive other than to build you up and help you find success in what you want to do.

Keep in mind, too, that your network doesn't have to be in your own backyard. You can network with people across the country, or even across the globe, through the Internet and social media. You can even use email or a phone to communicate. For that matter, you don't even have to communicate directly with them. You can follow them on Instagram, Facebook, Twitter, and LinkedIn. You can visit their websites and read their blogs, where you can gain information and insight into their success.

Books are also great mentors. Personal and professional development books will enhance your success a great deal. Industry-sensitive books that cover success strategies and techniques, as well as how-to books, can help you gain knowledge and expertise in any area. And don't forget memoirs and autobiographies—if you're a small business owner who wants to build an empire, read a book about the life of someone who did just that and wrote about it. You might not discover all of the strategies to their success, but you'll gain an incredible insight into their life, habits, goals, mistakes, and, yes, successes. In this way, you'll get a glimpse into a person's success, but also an awareness of the beliefs, values, and daily actions that made it happen. Sometimes, you'll find that your network's secrets to success aren't in what they did, but how they did it, what their motivation was, and their daily practices.

"Sometimes you have to fake it till you make it."

If You Can't Take Giant Steps, Take Little Steps

Isaac Newton's first Law of Motion states that an object in motion will stay in motion, but an object at rest will stay at rest, until there is action by an outside force. This is true not only for objects, but also for people. When applied to the pursuit of goals or dreams, inactivity becomes a chronic condition that can permanently disable a dream.

Sure, there are times when things might temporarily slow down or even halt for a short period. It's also true that when it comes to success and dreams, we tend to have little patience—we want it and we want it now! However, we can't always reach our success and dreams as fast as we wish. That's because everything cannot always be in our control. There might be challenges or obstacles that require you to take a step back. Maybe you'll even have to revert to Plan B. Financial issues might hold you up, or there might be familial or work obligations that require your attention. Those things happen, and when they do, it's not time for you to put that dream on a backburner and allow it to become a "someday" dream. Even if you can't do everything you want, you can do *something*.

You may be in a holding pattern or something beyond your control may be holding you back. It doesn't mean you have to stop moving toward your dream. If you cannot take a big step, you can take a series of small steps that will still move you closer to success.

Let's say you find that you have to wait several months before you can take a major step toward your goal. Maybe you have to complete a major, pressing project, or you might be waiting for investors or funds before you can launch a business. That doesn't mean that you have to halt all activities during this impasse. As a matter of fact, this is a great opportunity for you to make progress in other ways. It is an opportunity to take small steps that will make you better prepared for success.

For instance, this is the time for learning and soaking up everything we can about our business or success. And there is always something to learn—you might be quite skilled in your industry, but you might not be so skilled in all the aspects of running a business. You might not know anything about inventory software, payroll taxes, or employee laws. If so, this is the perfect time for you to do some studying and research.

You might not have the funds to sign a lease or purchase a printing press, but you might have $50 or $100 to register for a small business workshop, where you can learn about all aspects of small business management and network with other small business owners and experts.

You can find associations or groups that will be learning tools for you. You can start studying everything you need to know in the comfort of your own home. Seek websites and Internet courses and tutorials. Watch podcasts and read blogs. This is also an excellent time to network! While you're online, it's a good time to start looking for those positive people you want to surround yourself with.

Read and read and read!! Knowledge is the greatest success tool there is. Gain it. There are hundreds, okay, thousands, of books out there that show you what success looks like and the steps you must take to work toward your dream. This is the perfect time for you to read them.

While it might not seem like you are doing a lot, you are keeping your dream alive and in motion. The best part is you are taking steps that will improve your chances of success, and when added up, little steps can make great progress.

Don't forget, either, that everything you do, no matter how small, is capable of presenting to you yet another opportunity. Keep your eyes open and look for it.

Don't get frustrated if your goals are not moving fast enough. It is so easy to get swept up in frustration when there are delays or setbacks. It is disappointing when you face struggles, but don't forget that every delay or struggle sharpens your troubleshooting and problem-solving skills. It opens the door to creative thinking, as well. And even if your grand vision has to be scaled back for the time being, there is always the possibility that the setback will open the door to another, bigger opportunity.

"A smooth sea never made a skilled sailor," Franklin D. Roosevelt once said. You don't become an expert at anything until you're able to navigate through the roughest waters. But when you do, watch out! While others are too fearful to attempt the stormy sea, you'll know that you can handle what comes your way. You'll be able and ready to face and overcome any conditions or circumstances you encounter.

If you've had a setback or delay, don't use it as an excuse to take a seat. Instead, take a step, no matter how small to keep things in motion and your goal within your sight. Little steps taken consistently over time make as much progress as a big step taken occasionally.

And always remember, if you do something positive everyday toward your goals and dreams, you are a success. A little progress each day adds up to BIG results.

That's important to remember when the work ahead of you appears to be monumental or perhaps insurmountable. The thought of accomplishing all of it can be so overwhelming that it's difficult to know where to start. However, doing just one thing a day will ultimately achieve the results you want … and without the overwhelm. As they say, the best way to eat an elephant is one bite at a time. I know, we're not eating elephants here, but I think you get the correlation. A dream broken down into bite-size pieces is no longer a dream—it's a plan in action.

"Champions keep playing till they get it right."

Billie Jean King

Chapter Four

GET YOUR LIFE HEALTHY, SO YOU CAN MOVE ON

If you break your leg, it has to heal before you can climb a mountain. If you're exhausted, you have to sleep to regain your energy and be able to think clearly. Your body knows when you're ill or injured, and it sends you signs of discomfort or pain to tell you that something is wrong so you can tend to it and start the healing process. Poor health, whether it's physical, emotional, or mental health, impedes the ability to do just about anything in life. When you're not healthy, you cannot be at peak performance.

Just as the body has to be healthy to function at its best, so, too, do the heart, mind, and soul. Just as you have to be healthy to run a marathon, your inner and outer world have to be healthy in order for you to run your life.

What does that mean? It means that not only do you have to be healthy in order to enjoy an optimal life, but your life has to be healthy, as well. Every day, we are exposed to so much—some great, some good, and some bad. The world we live in can invite joy, happiness, love, and gratitude into our lives, but it can also include anxiety, anger, jealousy, revenge, and unhealthy temptations. In this segment of your journey, you will focus on removing the unhealthy toxins, attitudes, and people from your life so you can free yourself from their reins.

"My personal goals are to be happy, healthy and be surrounded by loved ones."

Kiana

Toxic Relationships Suck; Get Rid of Them

Everyone knows that toxic substances are unhealthy. Toxic substances in the water, air, or land do much more than pollute—they destroy our health and the environment. Knowing that environmental toxins are unhealthy, what happens when there are toxic people in our lives? They do the same—they destroy the lives of others and the health of our relationships.

To accomplish your goals and dreams, you must clean up your life of anything that is toxic. Like asbestos in a building, it must be removed, or at the very minimum, contained. If you have toxic and negative situations, you cannot move forward because these situations drain you and demand one hundred percent of your time and attention. Like a two-year-old child having a temper tantrum, toxic people must be addressed before you can continue with the task at hand. Too often, though, we tend to hope that if we ignore the situation, it will resolve itself or go away.

That is not going to happen. Just like oil spills in our oceans, toxic situations and relationships have to be addressed and cleaned up in order for them to go away. Otherwise, they can and will impact everything and everyone around them.

Often people think everything will fix itself once they gain success or accomplish their dreams. When I have money ... when I find the right person ... when I get a promotion ... then I will be happy, and nothing will affect me. I will be so happy that their misery, doubt, lack of trust, or negativity won't be able to touch me! The truth is entirely opposite of this belief. You must resolve whatever is unhealthy in your life in order to be happy.

Many people believe that they need to be rich to be happy. Then all of their troubles, anxieties, and fears will go away. They can do whatever they want to do, when they want to do it! However, research shows that rich people aren't happier—in other words, money cannot buy happiness. Neither can fame. If money doesn't make us happy, what does? There has been considerable research that reveals that the primary thing that makes us happy is the relationships in our lives ... but only when those relationships are healthy.

Now, let's look at how those relationships and toxic situations impact your ability to achieve your dreams. You cannot focus on your goals when there is havoc running rabid in your life. Those people or situations will drain you of your energy, positivity, and endurance. At a minimum, they are usually emotionally exhausting. At most, they can be toxic and paralyzing.

When you want to move forward and succeed, sometimes you must make a conscious decision of what you want your future to look like. It may mean leaving a person, relationship, job, or situation behind. It might mean changing careers entirely or moving across the country, where there are opportunities in your field.

There is also a possibility that you will have to take a deep look into your relationship with your significant other. If your partner or spouse doesn't support you or your dreams, you cannot focus on your dreams—you're too busy focusing on trying to appease them, convince them, or working silently behind the scenes on your dreams so they don't voice their disapproval and try to abolish your dreams altogether. If family members or friends try to discourage you, their negativity will affect you. If you're around people who don't have dreams, they will try to dissuade you from pursuing yours. Misery does love company.

From the time we are born, relationships have a huge impact on our lives. The people around us affect our attitudes and actions. Yes, you will be like the people you associate with the most. If you have friends and family members who thrive on drama, your life will be full of drama. It cannot help but seep into your life. Drama is a huge energy drainer. Success and chaos cannot survive together in the same environment at the same time. Like fire and water, they're exact opposites. You must separate yourself from that drama to focus on your success.

How do you do that? You can start by limiting time spent with negative friends. It's actually not uncommon to do this. People grow and change over time and can find that their interests, attitudes, and outlooks are no longer the same. In this case, it is easy to ease yourself out of the relationship. This happens during the natural course of life. Those who were your friends in grade school might not have been your friends in high school or college. Your best friend is now gainfully employed, married, and has two children, a house, and a dog. Your interests have changed … your lives have changed. The two of you didn't decide that you didn't want to see each other as often; life just happened.

If the toxic relationships involve family members, especially close family members, it is your responsibility to remove yourself from situations and discussions that cause stress, anxiety, negativity, or disagreements. Keep the conversations light and non-judgmental. Change the topic. Cut your visits short. The less opportunity toxic people have to impact your life, the more opportunity you will have to experience the life you want.

It sounds easy, doesn't it? What happens, though, when the toxic relationship in your life is the one you have with yourself? That sounds complicated, and it can be. The truth is we are often our own worst critic. We look in the mirror and see only our imperfections. We look into our souls and see our faults. We compare ourselves to others and, unfortunately, believe we fall short. For some reason, we stay true to our right to judge ourselves and spew harsher criticism on ourselves than we would ever dream of doing to others. We convince ourselves that we are not as good as, smart as, or deserving of what we want as the next person. We tell ourselves we are not good enough to find the success we want. We deem ourselves unworthy of achieving our dreams, so why even try?

The toxic relationship you have with yourself can result in excuses for what cannot be done. Those excuses provide you with an easy out, so you don't have to try. You can give up right here and now because it's not going to happen. You don't know enough to achieve success, or you don't have enough money to make your vision a reality. You might even tell yourself it's too much work, and you simply cannot do it.

When the relationship we have with our self is critical and flawed, it provides us with a built-in excuse for not succeeding, or even trying. Sometimes, we truly believe that our weaknesses or deterrents are valid and that they will hold us back. We will tell ourselves were not smart enough, we didn't go to college, we don't know enough. We believe that our future is limited because we don't have a college degree, nicely framed and prominently displayed on the wall. Regardless of the stories and falsehoods we use to sabotage our dreams, they do the job—snuffing out any spark or flame and our desire to prove ourselves deserving and worthy of the life we want. During this time of self-imposed criticism, we are toxic to our success—proof that if there's an anecdote to success, it's self-administered.

However, there can become a point when you don't want to settle anymore. You come to the realization that you didn't have to be imprisoned in a lifetime of lack of opportunities simply because you didn't receive a degree. Accepting that self-imposed limitation would have kept many people from becoming successful. Did you know that more than one-third of the world's billionaires don't have a college degree? Here are just a few names you might recognize: Steve Jobs, Bill Gates, and Mark Zuckerberg became household names without a college degree. So did Rachael Ray and Ellen DeGeneres. And let's not forget about the legendary success of Henry Ford and John D. Rockefeller. They seized opportunities that weren't dependent on their education or their industry. In every industry, there are billionaires who refused to let perceived limitations stop them from pursuing their dreams, including the technology, automotive, food, oil, real estate, entertainment, and financial industries.

Knowing that, I asked, "Why not me?" Why should I allow anything to hold me back from having a successful career or, for that matter, a successful life? This realization was a critical shift in thinking. Once I started telling myself, "I am smart enough; I can do this," the process of seeing my vision and recognizing my opportunities began.

It's all about your mindset. You can let limitations hold you back or you can use them to motivate yourself to prove them wrong. If you're someone who loves to prove someone wrong, take this opportunity to prove *yourself* wrong. Show yourself that you are capable of accomplishing what you want and that you are worthy of the success that others enjoy. I did, and the simple fact that I escaped an "it's not possible" mentality was what really made it possible.

Once you have a great career and successful life, there is a natural and spontaneous reaction—it requires you to change your thought process. You must tell yourself you deserve to meet your visions and goals. You need to firmly imbed that belief in your mind and use it as motivation. However, it's just as important that you realize something many people don't—just because you deserve success doesn't mean you are actually going to achieve it. Sitting on the couch and waiting for success to fall in your lap isn't going to happen. You have better chances of winning the lottery without buying a ticket. Simply stated, you cannot be a bystander to your own success. You have to be an active participant in your success, every single step of the way. You have to set goals and stick with your deadlines. You have to be positive and utilize every opportunity that comes your way. You have to make decisions and be accountable for their outcomes. It won't happen overnight, but it will happen.

The first and most important step is to get started, which can also be the hardest step for some. Something you can do and others do is a very simple tool, but it's one that works very well. Write yourself notes and tape them on the mirror in your bathroom. Every morning, read them while brushing your teeth, doing your hair, or putting on make-up. Make sure they are positive notes and affirmations that motivate you and remind you of your goals and your attributes. They could be as simple as "You're smart and energetic," or "You can do this." The notes you write as your daily affirmations and reminders will vary and be specific to your dreams and goals. It might seem cheesy, but it really does work. Famous people who will attest to the power of affirmations include Oprah Winfrey, Denzel Washington, and Jennifer Lopez. Let's not forget Jim Carrey, the once struggling aspiring actor who wrote himself a 10-million-dollar check "for acting services rendered," then carried it in his pocket for several years... until he actually had the 10 million dollars to cash it. This is proof that when you affirm your strengths and goals, opportunities begin to present themselves. Then, something powerful starts to happen—that something is success.

So, don't be toxic with yourself. Start believing in yourself and begin the process of creating a healthy relationship with the one person who matters most—yourself. Try putting a note on your mirror as a daily reminder that you are capable and worthy and put another on your nightstand, where you will see it first thing in the morning and the last thing at night. In this way, you will start and end your day with confidence.

A healthy life and healthy relationships depend on a healthy attitude and belief system. To have those, it's important that you understand that there are some things you cannot control, but there are some things that are only in your control.

You can always change yourself. You can change your visions, goals, and dreams. You can change your attitude and mindset. You can change your beliefs. You can change your perceptions. You can change your expectations. Even more important, you can change how you think of yourself. Your opinion matters, more than you know. Yet, people always seem to seek the opinion of others to validate their dreams, actions, thoughts, and opinions!

There are things you cannot change, too. Most important, you cannot change other people. You can't change their attitude, words, or actions. But the good news is, you can change your reaction to them and your exposure to them. Remember the wise words of Eleanor Roosevelt, "No one can make you feel inferior without your consent." Don't give people the permission or the opportunity to demean you or negatively impact your opinion of yourself. Sometimes the healthy thing to do is to let them go. You can't change the people around you, but you can change the people you CHOOSE to be around.

"Deliberately seek the company of people who influence you to think and act on building the life you desire. Let one of those people be you."

Napoleon Hill

Create New Daily Habits

We mistakenly fall into the trap of thinking of habits as bad things. She has a habit of putting herself down. She bites her fingernails and snacks when bored or stressed. He nervously jiggles the coins in his pocket or taps his fingers on his desk. When we think of habits, we think of things like smoking, procrastinating, overeating, impulsive spending, and spending too much time on social media. Yes, bad habits can have a negative effect in many areas of our lives, and they should be addressed. But did you know that habits aren't always bad? We can have good habits, too. Creating a (good) habit can actually be conducive to success!

Living a successful life means changing your habits so they conform with success, instead of conflicting with success.

Most likely, you have heard the phrase, "When in Rome, do as the Romans do." This means when you are in Rome, you should adopt their customs and their habits. Fit in with their culture and accept their lifestyle. In other words, become a Roman.

This advice works very well in the arena of success. If you want to be successful, adopt the customs and habits of successful people.

It is said that like attracts like. If there are successful people you admire and want to be like, do what they do to attract what they've attracted in their life. Purposely study the habits of the successful and implement them in your life. While everyone has different habits, there are some habits that are common among very successful people:

1. They get up early. Successful people start their day before most people. Some even claim to wake up three hours before their workday begins. They use this time wisely—by practicing other good habits, such as exercising and planning their day.

2. They are devout readers. Successful people read, and they read often. Billionaire Warren Buffett even claims that reading is the most critical habit in creating his success and wealth. The next time you want to binge watch the latest Netflix series, pick up a book instead. Read personal and professional development books, biographies of

successful people, and nonfiction books. Read books for ideas, education, self-improvement, and inspiration. Learning is one of the best success habits there is.

3. Become disciplined. Stop the bad habit of procrastinating, putting off success for another day and create a new habit of doing something every day to work toward your goals. Creating a to-do list can help. Break your goals into small steps and make it a daily habit to do one thing on that list every single day.

4. They schedule their day. In other words, don't let life take control of your schedule. Instead, live your life by the schedule you want. Prioritize your time, and you'll find yourself less likely to be affected by distractions. Mark Twain once said, "Eat a live frog first thing in the morning," meaning to do your hardest chore of the day the first thing in the morning. Once it's done, the rest of the day will look pretty good. You might even find that it's a breeze!

5. Get organized. Bestselling author Stephen King uses organization as a habit before he sits down to write. He consistently follows the same routine— he starts writing at the same time every day. He sits in the same chair, in the same office, to write.

He keeps his papers and desk organized in the same manner as they were the day before, and he turns on the same music. King claims that his preferred organization and daily ritual prepares him to focus on writing.

6. Repetition. Practice makes perfect. At the very least, it creates improvement. NBA champion Michael Jordan got cut from his high school basketball team and used that as incentive to practice—as much as five hours a day. Focus intently on perfecting your skill or craft for five hours a day, and you'll also be certain to see noticeable improvement.

7. Unplug. Take time away from work and discussing work. Intentionally set aside quiet time to think and meditate. You must clear your mind on occasion to continue to see your visions. Otherwise, it's like you're trying to see through the forest, but you can't—all you can see are the trees. Also, remember to unplug from your phone and social media from time to time. This is one of the biggest time consumers for many, and it keeps you from being fully involved in your own life. You cannot enjoy the life you have if you're too busy trying to find out what others are doing with their lives. It is also true that it is nearly impossible to

see any opportunities that present themselves when you're looking down at a phone.

8. Balance. Keep balance in your life. If you spend all your efforts and attentions on your professional success, you will miss your personal successes. They are easy to overlook and fall through the cracks. To be truly successful, you must share your attention and keep balance.

Do some research and discover the habits of successful people you admire. Then implement those habits in your life. The more you behave as a success, the more you will become successful. There are many books out there that talk about the habits of the successful. You must read *The 7 Habits of Highly Effective People* by Stephen Covey. I also recommend *The Power of Habit* by Charles Duhigg. Pour yourself into these and other books and learn everything you can. Successful people spend their time reading about success and the success of others. It's a habit you should adopt, as well.

This reminds me of something that happened when my boys were in junior high school. At the beginning of one semester, the boys came home and handed me the school's new dress code. This dress code now allowed the boys and girls to wear shorts to school, which they had never been allowed to do in the past. My response was, "Okay, now you get to wear your play clothes to school, but I wonder what you are now going to do at school." Well, in a short time, the administration found that they had twice as many issues with behavioral problems than before. My boys had more classroom notes sent home about misbehaving because the kids didn't feel like listening and learning— they were in their play clothes and wanted to play. It was only natural and the result of what they've always known and done. We have learned behaviors, and the type of clothing we wear does influence our behavior. So, start a habit of wearing the influence of successful behaviors.

It is said that we will be as successful as the five people we hang around the most. If we hang around with people who are pessimistic, we will become pessimistic. If we hang around with people who are lazy, we will become lazy right along with them. But if we associate with people who are driven and ambitious, we will also increase our drive and ambitions. If we hang around with people who are positive thinkers, we will also become more optimistic. If we hang around with successful people, guess what? That's right—we will adopt their habits and begin living the life of a successful person. We will begin to dress like them, act like them, and conduct ourselves like them.

Who do you spend your time with?

Whether that person is your next-door neighbor or the CEO of your company, let their habits change your habits. If you want to be the next Michael Jordan (and are tall enough), follow his daily practice ritual. In other words, if you "want to be like Mike," do the things Mike did to achieve success.

Replicate the daily habits of successful people so you can begin to replicate their success in your own life. Yes, you may have to break bad habits before you can create new habits. But habits can be broken, and new habits are just as easy to create as bad ones. All you have to do is make it a daily practice, done consistently over time. After all, that's how habits are formed.

There is a difference between associating with and adopting the habits of successful people and seeking their counsel. Successful people actively seek the counsel and wisdom of successful people. They find a mentor who can teach them what they know and share their experience with them.

When you're looking for a mentor, search for someone who has already accomplished what you want to do, not just someone who teaches the basic principles. Simply stated, learn from those who do, not those who talk. You want someone who has made mistakes and learned from them, someone who is willing to share the principles and practices behind their success.

Most mentors are passionate about what they do. They want to help you succeed. The mentors in my life have shared the secrets of their industry, but they've also shared the important principles behind their success. One common principle among them is that they are firm believers in planning. They don't wing it and hope for the best. No, they create a step-by-step plan for every endeavor they attempt. They don't leave success to chance, choosing instead to follow the advice of Benjamin Franklin, who said, "If you fail to plan, you are planning to fail."

However, they also know that planning isn't everything—even the best laid plans can fail. That's why successful people have learned to rely on their instincts. They pay attention to their gut and give their instincts real credence, weighing them and determining the underlying issues behind why that instinct is good or bad. Our instincts are there for a reason. When they present themselves, don't shove them back down. Take time to determine if they have real merit. If they do, have the confidence to believe those gut instincts. They're trying to tell you something.

Successful people also know that there will be setbacks on every journey. There will be times when we come up short or even fail. Remember, we are all human, and we make mistakes. When we set out to pursue a goal, there is no such thing as hindsight to guide us. Therefore, do what successful people would do—don't give up. That's a surefire way to make sure you won't succeed. Just because you have a bad day or revert to an old, unhealthy habit, that doesn't mean that you can't start over the next day.

The past is behind you, and you can't change it. Don't dwell on it, and don't give it the power to wreck today. Forget about it and start anew. Your future is in front of you, and you'll never get to it by going in reverse.

Habit:
"The intersection of knowledge, skill and desire."

Stephen R. Covey

Improving Your Life Situations

A large piece of action for successful people is that they are constantly working on improving. That includes their personal life and business life. They can recognize and see opportunities that will benefit others and themselves. Because they have a vision and a set of goals, they can see an opportunity very well. Success is never done. There are always new challenges and goals.

Apple is a great example. Before a new iPhone is launched, they are already busy determining how to make their next smartphone faster, better, and more user friendly. They develop new, improved features, with increased capacity and speed. If their product falls behind the competition in any area, they are constantly at work to address the issue and stay in the forefront of the industry.

If we sit still, someone, somewhere will pass us up. The continual process of improvement, whether it is improving our mindset or our product or service, is a key component to not only achieving success, but also in sustaining it.

Successful people also know that credibility is key to their success. This can be credibility in many different forms. Paying your debts on time, maintaining a good credit score, following through on commitments, doing what you say you will do, and treating others respectfully. Now I can tell you that many of us didn't start out this way. You don't have to have a great credit report to be successful, although with success, that usually comes in time. But you can change your financial habits and credit rating by honoring your financial responsibilities and payment plans starting today. This is changing your life situation and putting you on the path to do better and be better. This can take time; for that reason, it should not deter you from your dreams and goals. It could just mean it's another hurdle to overcome. In that case, get started on rebuilding your credibility today. You can do it with persistence and goals.

It's all about being accountable and creating the all-important trust that's vital to success.

> *"Promise only what you can deliver, then deliver more than you promise."*

Successful people also understand the importance of their family and personal time. If you ignore that to for the purpose of investing more into your business or work, you will suffer, and your family will be hurt as a result. You must thrive to improve all areas of your life—improving company situations for your employees, family and home improvements, and self-improvement. A successful person never stops trying to improve themselves to be the most they can be for themselves and their loved ones.

> *"Time can be an ally or an enemy. What it becomes depends entirely up to you, your goals, and your determination to use every available minute."*
>
> Zig Ziglar

Chapter Five

GOALS? YOU BET!
GOALS MAKE US WHO WE ARE

Trash Your List and Set Goals

Lists are good for going grocery shopping or buying Christmas presents, but to become the success you want to be, you must have goals. There are differences between a list and goals. Goals have timelines, but lists do not. Goals have achievements, and lists have tasks. Goals must be measurable and obtainable. Lists are nothing more than notes—basic to-do lists without a step-by-step plan.

1. We hear about goals all of the time. People ask us what our goals are, and they tell us to set them. However, it is rare that anyone tells us how they really work … and what it takes to make them work. But as any successful person will tell you, they are fantastic success tools that will help you

get started and make progress at a steady pace. Knowing that, it's very surprising that few people really know how to utilize goals.

2. Goals are very powerful because they are the pathway to your success. As you reach one goal, you will find another that you need to achieve. Goals will also change at times, depending on where your path in life is headed. Don't be afraid to change your goals if they do not apply to your dreams any longer. Our life and dreams are always changing, and new goals will be necessary.

3. A DREAM is a series of GOALS. A GOAL without a plan is just a wish.

4. A goal is a timed process that will make it possible for you to reach your desired dreams or visions. You need a vivid picture of what your dreams look like. Each part of the dream or vision will have its own goal. Dissect the dream or vision so you can put a timeline on each goal.

"When you set a timeline to your dreams,

you're setting your goals."

Goals are an absolute necessity for success. You must have a road map in order to move forward, to get to the next step. Goals are road maps, with specific destinations along the way. They are the plan for your dreams and visions in the future.

Most people have a tendency to procrastinate. It's just seems to make life easier to delay doing something, saving it for tomorrow or another day. I must admit I was the very worst at putting things off. As a result, I was always reacting to situations that occurred because I put something off … until the time I came face to face with an issue that needed to finally be addressed and I was forced to act. Being reactive, rather than proactive, is a stressful way to live daily, and it is not productive.

One of the things you need to do to be successful is face your faults and change them. I knew I had to change this negative habit if I were going to succeed. To help me do that, I started writing a "Things to Do" list; and as I finished a task, I checked it off the list. Wow!! You wouldn't think that would be a big deal, but it was. I was ecstatic when I could check something off the list. I found this worked very well for me as a motivator. Once I changed that habit, I realized I needed goals to meet the needs of my dreams for the future.

Meeting each of my goals is very satisfying for me and leads me to my next success. My goals move around and change frequently. Just because you set up your goals, that doesn't mean you can't deviate from them. Circumstances change and so does life. Life has a way of turning left when you thought you were going to turn right. Our vision, too, will change as we grow and find our opportunities.

When I was younger, I would have never guessed in a million years I would be sitting here at 5:00 a.m. writing a book. I wouldn't have guessed I would be serving others with the wisdom I have learned over the years. I wouldn't have believed I would be a multi-millionaire. Life can take us to places we could only dream of in our imagination — that is, until we set goals and it becomes a reality.

"A dream doesn't become reality through magic; it takes sweat, determination, and hard work."

Colin Powell

Chapter Six

COURAGE IS TO START, THE REST WILL COME

Now What?

It's time for action. You now know what it is you want, and you're ready to go get it. Don't wait for the perfect time, because it will never come. Nothing comes without action. Follow your goals and change them when appropriate. Remember, goals are forever changing. As you complete one, another will take its place.

While you're moving forward, stay alert, always remembering to look at every situation in your life and find the opportunity in it. Look for the opportunity in your job, other jobs, business, other businesses, and in your personal life. They will come from everywhere.

Sometimes opportunity lets itself be known, loud and clear. It might be a phone call or a knock on the door.

Maybe it's an invitation to do something you've never done before. You don't know what will happen if you accept ... but you do know what will happen if you don't answer the door or accept the invitation—nothing.

One of the reasons we turn away from the opportunities that present themselves is because they come at inconvenient times or are disguised as something that looks like work. Yes, that four-letter word that stands between us and the things we want in life is one of the biggest reasons people don't recognize or grab the opportunities that come their way. When that happens, take a deeper look at the opportunity. Instead of saying, "What happens if it doesn't work out?," ask yourself what could happen if it does work out! Accepting an invitation to go out with friends might connect you with a potential employer, a new customer, or perhaps, your future spouse.

But what happens when the opportunity actually scares you? It might require you to take a giant leap of faith or step far, far out of your comfort zone. Maybe it has the potential to be life changing. If the opportunity frightens you, that doesn't mean that you should run away from it. It means that it's time to stop and take a second look—it just might be something big.

Whenever an opportunity creates a major emotional response, it's trying to get your attention. However, when the response is fear, we do what we've always done and steer clear of it. But what if that fear is there to get your attention and make sure this isn't just another opportunity that you don't pay attention to? What if being afraid is the way an opportunity screams at you and says, "Hey, wake up! Pay attention! This is important!"

Now, there are times when something is so big that it scares you for other reasons—the risk is extremely high, there is potential danger, or the change can be greater than you really want. In that case, your fear might be trying to protect you. The mind and body have protective mechanisms, so heed the warning and do your research. Determine if this is something you really want … and if the risk is worth it.

On the other hand, there are opportunities and ideas that grab onto you and won't let go. You might push them aside, but they come right back. They nag at the back of your mind and leave you wondering, *What if?* Maybe they keep presenting themselves again and again, giving you a second and a third chance to say yes. They're no longer hiding in the weeds—they're raising their head and hissing loudly, saying here I am! Look at me! Persistent, returning ideas and opportunities are trying to tell you something. When opportunity speaks this loudly, listen.

Yes, opportunity can be frightening. It can cause anxiety. What if it doesn't work? What if it will change your life forever? Often, the things we want the most are also the things that scare us the most. Uncertainty also causes fear, even when the outcome might be positive. Unfortunately, though, we've been trained to perceive fear as a negative emotion—step back, don't get close, protect yourself, remove yourself from this scary thing immediately! Before you turn your back and run far into the sunset, leaving that opportunity in the dust, ask yourself if you are in real danger or if you're just stepping out of your comfort zone.

Sometimes, your fear is nothing more than an indicator that something important could happen ... if you let it. But every time you let yourself face fear and get the results you want, you're actually achieving a new level in your growth.

Sometimes fear can come from a sense of urgency, too. There will be times when opportunity presents itself and you'll know that you must act quickly, or you will the opportunity forever. Yes, opportunity has a way of raising its head long enough to be noticed ... but it doesn't stick around indefinitely. And there is no reassurance that the same opportunity will ever return—one reason why waiting for the "right" opportunity might not be a good idea. Perhaps, the opportunity that's right in front of you right now will lead you to the right opportunity down the road—but only if you take it.

For that reason, do what you can to overcome your fear. When you were young, you didn't let fear stop you. You fell when taking your first steps, but you get back up. It was scary when the training wheels came off your bike, but you learned how to balance yourself. You might have changed schools. You left high school and entered college or the workplace. Perhaps, you even bought your first car or took out your first loan. There are many things in life that cause fear ,,, and history tells us that it was scary at first, but not for long.

Facing your fear will give you confidence. You will then have the confidence to move forward with your dreams and goals. You will trip here and there but that will just teach you a lesson and you'll keep on moving. Keep moving toward your dreams, no matter how big or small the opportunity is. It's still moving forward, and that's the right direction! Sure, we don't always get there as fast as we want, but as long as we continue moving forward, we will reach our dreams.

Remember that you also must think out of the box. Find solutions to problems, and it will carry you so much further than the person who sees the problem and walks away. Successful people are problem solvers. Instead of running from the problem, they take action and find a way to solve the problem. They don't let problems get in their way or stop them from their goals and dreams. Problems in successful people's lives are called opportunities!

"I attribute my success to this: I never gave or took an excuse."

Florence Nightingale, founder of modern nursing

Chapter Seven

BE KIND!

Many people think you have to flex muscles to win or to get what you want, but that's not true. People who bully their way to what they want, do so because they are not confident in their ability to reach their goals and dreams. If you stay on track and be kind to people, you will be more powerful than others. Even if you must bid or compete for a job or project, do it in a kind and respectful way. No one likes a successful person who boasts and looks down on others.

Respect everyone in your path, whether they serve you food at a restaurant or they are billionaires. They are all trying to survive and take care of their needs. Don't be stingy with your money and time, help others. Find a charity that is dear to your heart. We all have been touched with loved ones who have been sick or have had troubles in their life. Don't overlook them. When you reach your success and dreams, it's your responsibility to help others. Choose to be kind over being right, and you will be right every time because kindness is a sign of strength.

---

*"You have two hands,
one for helping yourself
and one for helping others."*

Chapter Eight

THE AHA! MOMENT

As we've discussed, opportunity is always there—we just can't see it. It might be subtle, or it might be so present in our lives that others would question why we didn't see it sooner—yes, the old "if it was a snake, it would have bit you" scenario.

The fact is, we get so used to our surroundings and routines that sometimes our mind has to travel a bit outside of its regular mode to become aware and allow us to see something in a different way. This chapter will give you ideas and examples of ways to find opportunities ... and create them.

Finding Opportunities

The strange thing about opportunity is that it can often come to us an idea. Out of the blue, we get an idea and say,

"Hey, why can't this be done differently?" or "Why hasn't someone thought of a better way?"

Guess what? That's an opportunity. Your mind is on to something, and it's trying to tell you to do something about it. The seed has been planted, but it's up to you to nurture it and bring it to harvest.

Oftentimes, this can occur as a result of our everyday life. At work, we might struggle with doing something tedious and that just takes too long. Then we get an idea of how the process can be streamlined or improved. That's an opportunity.

Medical practitioners treat patients, but they are in a unique position to identify shortcomings in devices or products. Sometimes, they see that there is need for a new product or device altogether. Their experience and expertise open the door to opportunity to idealize and invent that device or product and help people across the world.

Glasses for color blind people are an example. Someone had to think of those and know enough about the eye and the color spectrum and deficits to conceptualize and create glasses that let individuals see the world in color for the first time. Thank goodness, someone had the idea and seized the opportunity.

Let's look at a few examples of people like you and me, who found opportunity at unlikely times and through different ways.

Questions

Sometimes, when you ask yourself a question, other people want the answers, too. That's an opportunity waiting to be answered. Often, these questions begin with phrases like, "I wonder ..."

Chris Englert found opportunity in two ways. First, she worked in higher education publishing, an industry that was declining. Knowing her job would end, she was on the lookout for a different career. She had always loved traveling and had even started her own travel blog. One day, while sitting in her living room looking at trail maps of Denver, she noticed trails and said, "I wonder where those trails go?" The second question was her Aha moment, "I wonder who else might want to know?"

Chris founded Eat Walk Learn and is the author of Denver's most popular hiking and park books. And she did all of this because 1) a potential job loss made her open her eyes to other opportunities, and 2) she answered a random question that popped into her mind.

Chris also believes that hobbies are the key to opportunity. She now advises others to create a business out of their three favorite things. She did, which is why she named her business Eat Walk Learn.

Hobbies and Pastimes

K.J. Kruk had a real estate and hospitality business when she got the idea to write a story. As a child, it was something she enjoyed doing. This story line was so unique that she started writing it right away, before she forgot any part of it. Eventually, the story came to an end … and that's when K.J. realized that she had written a children's book—one that actually might be worth publishing. Her book, Leo Gray and the Lunar Eclipse, became a bestseller among middle-grade students. Today, Kruk is a full-time author and illustrator.

It is the author and illustrator of the acclaimed middle-grade novel Leo Gray and the Lunar Eclipse.

Identify Unmet Needs

Who would have thought that a simple, heart-wrenching, statement by a small child would turn your life around? It did just that for Katie Blomquist, a teacher. A boy in her first-grade class asked her for a bike for his birthday because he didn't have one. Being a teacher, she didn't make enough money to buy him a bike, but she wanted to do something. So, she started a GoFundMe that raised more than $80,000 and was able to buy a new bike, lock, and helmet for every one of the 650 students in her school. Mission accomplished, she knew could help more children if she continued, so she quit her job and started Going

Places, a nonprofit that allows her to touch more lives and make a greater mark on the world.

Is there an unmet need around you? What can you do about it?

Turning Negatives into Positives

Carla Lyles wasn't the best student. She was also quiet, reserved, and often unhappy. That didn't change as she grew older. Unhappy at work and frequently changing jobs, she suffered from depression. When she became diagnosed with major depressive disorder, she quit work and started making hand-crafted greeting cards as a form of therapy. Today, she owns Carla Sue Greeting Cards and Gifts and has a successful business designing cards that contain positive, empowering messages.

Proof that sometimes opportunity is the silver lining in every dark cloud. Opportunity abounds. It's that question you need to know the answer to … the need that everyone else leaves unanswered … the job loss that makes you open your eyes to the world around you.

It's there. Stop. Look. Listen.

Then go out and seize it and make it yours.

STUDIES FOR SUCCESS

Ninety-two percent of people who set New Year goals never achieve them, only eight percent do and are in a category of goal-achievers. What do the goal achievers do different?

1. They begin with the end in mind; they know what the final destination is.
2. They build a support system around them.
3. They set specific and challenging goals.
4. They recognize when they're procrastinating.
5. They practice the 52 and 17 rule, when working on goals, spend 52 minutes on goals and followed by 17 minutes of rest.
6. They listen to music for focus.
7. They don't multi-task.

University of Scranton

Four skills make the most successful businesspeople, if you are headed to your dreams and success, you have these skills:

1. Self-awareness
2. Self-management
3. Social awareness
4. Relationship management

Dr. Travis Bradberry

I BELIEVE IN PINK

I believe … laughing is the best calorie burner.

I believe … in kissing, kissing a lot.

I believe … in being strong, when everything else is wrong.

I believe … happy girls are the prettiest.

I believe … tomorrow is another day.

I believe … in miracles.

Audrey Hepburn

ABOUT THE AUTHOR

Bonnie Fallin is an opportunity expert, multimillionaire business entrepreneur, and the owner of multiple businesses, She is a public speaker, author, mentor, and a real estate investor and stock market investor.

Bonnie opened her first business in 1991, In 1994, she sold it for a nice profit and entered the real estate industry. By 1997, she had bought her first real estate investment property, In 2006, she had the OPPORTUNITY to invest into several other businesses, making them the largest of their kind in Texas. After investing for another decade, she was blessed to have the OPPORTUNITY to do what she had desired for years, helping others achieve success by recognizing the OPPORTUNITIES around them.

What did it take? According to Bonnie:

I really had to be clear on what I wanted and how I would continue in a process to help others.

Today, Bonnie wants to help others succeed and achieve their dreams. She teaches others how to look for the OPPORTUNTIES that are around them on a day to day basis and shows them how to put on their OPPORTUNITY GLASSES and see them.

She now has combined her impressive experience in building a multimillion dollar business and strong mentoring into a mentoring program and specialty events program for entrepreneurs and executives, with her company, Opportunity Specs.

Bonnie is looking forward to the OPPORTUNITY to coach and lead you to your greatest dreams, by showing you the OPPORTUNITIES surrounding you.

www.ingramcontent.com/pod-product-compliance
Lightning Source LLC
LaVergne TN
LVHW011426080426
835512LV00005B/285